T0372566

PRAISE FOR
POETRY IS NOT A LUXURY

"An enduring and expertly curated anthology journeying through the seasonal movements of Summer, Autumn, Winter, and Spring. From Audre Lorde to Jean Valentine to Mosab Abu Toha—these are the poets you long to have in conversation with each other, and by some well-considered (and anonymous) miracle they have been assembled in shared rooms organized by time, and we have been granted generous entrance to listen, and to wait . . ."
—Cole Arthur Riley, author of *This Here Flesh*

"A perfect curation of incredible poets. I have no doubt that if you allow this book to be your constant companion, you will smile, cry, and certainly feel less alone in whatever you may be going through."
—Cleo Wade, #1 *New York Times* bestselling author of *Remember Love*

"*Poetry Is Not a Luxury* has been an invaluable resource for me the last few years and has introduced me to some of my favorite poems, such as 'Meditations in an Emergency' by Cameron Awkward-Rich and 'I Am the Horse' by Dorothea Lasky. Poetry curation seems to be an eye for feeling—an understanding of what the moment needs, and how to provide solace or meaning. *Poetry Is Not a Luxury* does that with incredible care in this collection. Every poem is a revelation."
—Florence Welch

POETRY IS NOT A LUXURY

POEMS FOR ALL SEASONS

EDITED BY THE CURATOR OF
@POETRYISNOTALUXURY ON INSTAGRAM

WASHINGTON
SQUARE PRESS

ATRIA

New York   Amsterdam/Antwerp   London
Toronto   Sydney/Melbourne   New Delhi

An Imprint of Simon & Schuster, LLC
1230 Avenue of the Americas
New York, NY 10020

For more than 100 years, Simon & Schuster has championed authors and the stories they create. By respecting the copyright of an author's intellectual property, you enable Simon & Schuster and the author to continue publishing exceptional books for years to come. We thank you for supporting the author's copyright by purchasing an authorized edition of this book.

No amount of this book may be reproduced or stored in any format, nor may it be uploaded to any website, database, language-learning model, or other repository, retrieval, or artificial intelligence system without express permission. All rights reserved. Inquiries may be directed to Simon & Schuster, 1230 Avenue of the Americas, New York, NY 10020 or permissions@simonandschuster.com.

Copyright © 2025 by @poetryisnotaluxury

All rights reserved, including the right to reproduce this book
or portions thereof in any form whatsoever. For information,
address Atria Books Subsidiary Rights Department,
1230 Avenue of the Americas, New York, NY 10020.

First Washington Square Press/Atria Books hardcover edition May 2025

WASHINGTON SQUARE PRESS / ATRIA BOOKS and colophon are registered trademarks of Simon & Schuster, LLC

Simon & Schuster strongly believes in freedom of expression and stands against censorship in all its forms. For more information, visit BooksBelong.com.

For information about special discounts for bulk purchases,
please contact Simon & Schuster Special Sales at 1-866-506-1949
or business@simonandschuster.com.

The Simon & Schuster Speakers Bureau can bring authors
to your live event. For more information, or to book an event,
contact the Simon & Schuster Speakers Bureau at 1-866-248-3049
or visit our website at www.simonspeakers.com.

Interior design by Lexy East

Manufactured in the United States of America

1   3   5   7   9   10   8   6   4   2

Library of Congress Control Number: 2024058367
ISBN 978-1-6680-6255-5
ISBN 978-1-6680-6256-2 (ebook)

For Audre Lorde

CONTENTS

INTRODUCTION

"Poetry is not a luxury." These words written by Audre Lorde are to me some of the most powerful words in prose ever penned. She writes on to explain that poetry "is a vital necessity of our existence. It forms the quality of the light within which we predicate our hopes and dreams toward survival and change, first made into language, then into idea, then into tangible action."[1] I chose her words as the name of my Instagram account hoping to shine a bright light on these truths, hoping to bring Audre Lorde and her lasting legacy to the forefront.

Lorde wrote of the revolutionary potential of poetry in 1977, and every day I continue to believe in the potential for poetry to shape the future. The poems gathered in this collection teach us to move toward change.

The poems are framed by the seasons to illuminate and celebrate the "beauty in every degree of flourishing," as Linda Gregg writes in her poem "Praising Spring."

---

[1] "Poetry Is Not a Luxury," by Audre Lorde, first published in *Chrysalis: A Magazine of Female Culture*, no. 3, 1977.

The poems remind us to take part in a more communal experience of the world. To say "*Thank You*" with Ross Gay as we find ourselves "half naked and barefoot in the frosty grass." Throughout, the poems honor how feelings survive and flourish. As each year "the seasons know exactly when to change,"[2] we are guided by the seasons: as they change, we are changing too.

This anthology, deeply inspired by Lorde's words, is a mixtape I made for you. If you are like me, you will find yourself returning to these poems as safe house when in need, to sing along, to be broken open, to recoup the energy you require to return to the world. Poetry holds all that is radiant and real—each line is a pattern we can feel and return to again and again. Let this book carry you as you travel through the years to come, through personal and collective joy and grief.

I invite you to let this collection of poetry nourish you and surprise you and change your life, to be your companion, to show you every possibility. As Brenda Shaughnessy writes, "We can read us. We are not alone."

Thank you for coming to these pages with me.

---

[2]"As" by Stevie Wonder from the album *Songs in the Key of Life*, Tamla Records, 1976.

POETRY IS NOT A LUXURY

SUMMER

One Heart
Li-Young Lee

Look at the birds. Even flying
is born

out of nothing. The first sky
is inside you, open

at either end of day.
The work of wings

was always freedom, fastening
one heart to every falling thing.

/'mīgrənt/

Tiana Nobile

Of an animal, especially a bird. A wandering species
whom no seas nor places limit. A seed who survives despite
the depths of hard winter. The ripple of a herring

steering her band from icy seas to warmer strands.
To find the usual watering-places despite
the gauze of death that shrouds our eyes

is a breathtaking feat. Do you ever wonder why
we felt like happy birds brushing our feathers
on the tips of leaves? How we lifted our toes

from one sandbank and landed—fingertips first—
on another? Why we clutched the dumb and tiny creatures
of flower and blade and sod between our budding fists?

From an origin of buried seeds emerge
these many-banded dagger wings.
We, of the sky, the dirt, and the sea. We,

the seven-league-booters and the little-by-littlers.
We, transmigrated souls, will prevail.
We will carry ourselves into the realms of light.

Idea

Kate Baer

I will enjoy this life. I will open it
like a peach in season, suck the juice
from every finger, run my tongue over
my chin. I will not worry about clichés
or uninvited guests peering in my windows.
I will love and be loved. Save and be saved
a thousand times. I will let the want into
my body, bless the heat under my skin.
My life, I will not waste it. I will enjoy this life.

The Love Cook

Ron Padgett

Let me cook you some dinner.
Sit down and take off your shoes
and socks and in fact the rest
of your clothes, have a daiquiri,
turn on some music and dance
around the house, inside and out,
it's night and the neighbors
are sleeping, those dolts, and
the stars are shining bright,
and I've got the burners lit
for you, you hungry thing.

The ways of the many

Aja Monet

you rise a witch bleeding gently in morning
fanning flies from fruit
you slice an avocado open and spoon the pit out
sprinkle sea salt and cayenne pepper
put a pot to boil on the stove
stuff sage and rosebud in a strainer
your hair is messy, eye boogers in the corners
you smell like a sleeping beauty who sweat
her kinks out in the second coming
like sticky dates in soiled hands
olive and enchanted
like bronzed blood panties
washed and hung from a clothesline midafternoon
you are a wildflower just after a thunderstorm
guava juice dripping on a chin
you are what is graceless
hardly regal before noon

Strawberry Moon

Franny Choi

The house was filled with the smell of it, the last misshapen, sweet-heavy berries of the season losing their shapes on the stove. The house was filled with the smell of fruit unbecoming, fruit pulled to its knees at fire's feet. All summer long, the bushes had whispered, *Take me*, shown us all the places we could kiss if we wanted. And so, as the light died, we put our mouths on the least lovable, the too-full, the easy-bruised, we shouted, *I choose you, and you, and you, and you*, and canned that hunger, and spooned it into our mouths on the coldest days.

On Seeing and Being Seen

Ama Codjoe

I don't like being photographed. When we kissed
at a wedding, the night grew long and luminous.
You unhooked my bra. *A photograph*
passes for proof, Sontag says, *that a given thing*
has happened. Or you leaned back to watch
as I eased the straps from my shoulders.
Hooks and eyes. Right now, my breasts
are too tender to be touched. *Their breasts*
were horrifying, Elizabeth Bishop writes. Tell her
someone wanted to touch them. I am touching
the photograph of my last seduction. It is as slick
as a magazine page, as dark as a street
darkened by rain. When I want to remember
something beautiful, instead of taking
a photograph, I close my eyes.
I watched as you covered my nipple
with your mouth. Desire made you
beautiful. I closed my eyes.
Tonight, I am alone in my tenderness.
There is nothing in my hand except a certain
grasping. In my mind's eye, I am
stroking your hair with damp fingertips. This is exactly
how it happened. On the lit-up hotel bed,
I remember thinking, My body is a lens
I can look through with my mind.

Cento for the Night I Said, "I Love You"

Nicole Sealey

Today, gentle reader,
is as good a place to start.
But you knew that, didn't you? Then let us
give ourselves over to the noise
of a great scheme that included everything.
That indicts everything.
Let us roam the night, together,
in an attempt to catch the stars that drop.

• • •

White clouds against sky
come humming toward me.
One closely resembling the beginning
of a miracle. There's
the moonlight on a curved path
lighting the purple flowers of fragrant June.
I dreamed him and there he was
silent as destiny,
lit by a momentary match.

• • •

Men are so clueless sometimes,
like startled fish
living just to live.
We are dying quickly
but behave as good guests should:

patiently allowing the night
to have the last word.
And I just don't know,
you know? I never had a whole lot to say
while talking to strange men.

• • •

What allows some strangers to go past strangeness? Exchanging
yearning for permanence. And who wouldn't
come back to bed? Love—
How free we are; how bound. Put here in love's name:
called *John*. A name so common as
a name sung quietly from somewhere.
Like a cry abandoned someplace
in a city about which I know.

• • •

Like black birds pushing against glass,
I didn't hold myself back. I gave in completely and went
all the way to the vague influence of the distant stars.
I saw something like an angel
spread across the horizon like some dreadful prophecy
refusing to be contained, to accept limits.
She said, "Are you sure you know what you're doing?"

• • •

I love you, I say, desperate
to admit that
the flesh extends its vanity
to an unknown land

where all the wild swarm.
This is not death. It is something safer,
almost made of air—
I think they call it *god*.

• • •

And it came to pass that meaning faltered, came detached.
I learned my name was not my name.
I was not myself. Myself
resembles something else
that had nothing to do with me, except
I am again the child with too many questions
as old as light. I am always learning the same thing:
one day all this will only be memory.
One day soon. For no good reason.

• • •

Some say we're lucky to be alive, to have
a sky that stays there. Above.
And I suppose I would have to agree . . .
but the hell with that.
It isn't ordinary. The way the world unravels,
from a distance, can look like pain
eager as penned-in horses.

• • •

Dying is simple—
the body relaxes inside
hysterical light
as someone drafts an elegy

in a body too much alive.
Love is like this;
not a heartbeat, but a moan.

• • •

One life is not enough
to remember all the things
marriage is. This town at dawn
can will away my lust
to suck honey from the sunlight,
so why am I out here trying
to make men tremble who never weep?

• • •

Can you see me
sinking out of sight
in the middle of our life?
Should I be ashamed of myself
for something I didn't know I—
(He walks by. He walks by
laughing at me.)
"What else did you expect
from this day forward?" *For better.* (Or worse.)

• • •

After all's said and after all's done
and all arrogance dismissed,
the distance rumbles in
sparing only stars.
The moon, like a flower,

survives as opinion
making it almost transparent.
The pieces of heavy sky
heavy as sleep.
I close my eyes
and this is my life now.

I went

C. P. Cavafy

I did not tether myself. I let go entirely and went,
I went into the luminous night,
to those pleasures that were half real,
and half wheeling in my brain.
And I drank of potent wines, as only the
valiant of voluptuousness drink.

Translated by Rae Dalven

Loveable

Raymond Antrobus

The first time you told me you loved me
I didn't say it back,

which is to say
that I was not loveable.

Those who have loved me before say
I made them feel second to some dream I was having.

You know the thing with dreams
you're the only one that sees them

so when I say I didn't know what was talking
the first night you said you loved me I mean

I needed to hear it in the morning
hear it said when neither of us

could be anyone
except who we are

Tired of Love Poems

Megan Fernandes

But we never tire of them, do we?
We wish to worship more than just each other.
We put a god first, sometimes a tree,
write a sonnet to a bird in the black
of night or offer a light to a stranger
and not call it love. But it is. To pull
out a chair is more than manners.
What we tire of is that we never tire of it.
How it guts us. How it fails, then reappears.
Because what is the bird compared to you?
The bird is replaced each morning.
You approach on a red bike in summer
and the poem takes shape. I entitle it
anything but Love, anything but what it is.

Tin Bucket

Jenny George

The world is not simple.
Anyone will tell you.
But have you ever washed a person's hair
over a tin bucket,
gently twisting the rope of it
to wring the water out?
At the end of everything,
dancers just use air as their material.
A voice keeps singing even
without an instrument.
You make your fingers into a comb.

Happiness

Mary Ruefle

Summer late evening

my friend the sunset

to surprise me

took the most interesting streets

Late he was

Longer than ever before

Ode to hunger

Zeina Hashem Beck

How I crave the strawberries
we bought on a road
in Cyprus the day we got married.
Their scent was divine & we forgot

to eat them.

Pattern

Garous Abdolmalekian

Your dress waving in the wind.
This
is the only flag I love.

At a Waterfall, Reykjavik

Eileen Myles

I still feel like
the world
is a piece
of bread

I'm holding
out half
to you.

Summer Solstice

Jenny Zhang

will be significant

im going to release something

soft and radiant

and true

into the world

Think of Others

M a h m o u d   D a r w i s h

As you prepare your breakfast, think of others
   (do not forget the pigeon's food).

As you conduct your wars, think of others
   (do not forget those who seek peace).

As you pay your water bill, think of others
   (those who are nursed by clouds).

As you return home, to your home, think of others
   (do not forget the people of the camps).

As you sleep and count the stars, think of others
   (those who have nowhere to sleep).

As you liberate yourself in metaphor, think of others
   (those who have lost the right to speak).

As you think of others far away, think of yourself
   (say: *If only I were a candle in the dark*).

43

Robin Coste Lewis

Absolutely nothing
significant
except the growing
realization that
with or without me
it is happening.
And that for
the first 42
I thought that
it needed my
approval, my agreement.
It began a while ago.
It's been waiting
and not waiting
wishing
I would catch up.
I am catching up
to the day
accepting
that the Sun cares
and does not care,
that with or without me
it will spin and burn.
That I should
spin and burn
too.

Jupiter

Nicholas Hogg

You get a moment,
sometimes, to consider the space
between planets. I open the window
while taking a bath, floating in the clear night sky
with Jupiter. Naked,
the two of us
in orbit.

Ode

Noor Hindi

Edgewater Beach, 2019
for Kevin

The night, so warm I could fall in love
with anything
including myself. My loves, you are the only people
I'd surrender my softness to.
The moon so blue. What's gold
is gold. What's real
is us despite
a country so grieved, so woke, so deathly.
Our gloom as loud as shells.
Listen. Even the ocean begs.
Put your hands in the sand, my friend.
It's best we bury ourselves.
What's heavy. What's heavy?
Becomes light.

Tender

Sophie Klahr

I spend late morning weeping with the news:
a black bear with burnt paws is euthanized
along the latest wildfire's newest edge.
It was crawling on its forearms, seeking
a place to rest. I Google more; reports
leak out: the bear had bedded down behind
a house, below a pine, to lick its paws.
In hours before its end, officials named
it Tenderfoot, though some reports report
just Tender. Later, I will teach a class
where we'll discuss the lengths of lines in poems.
I'll say a sonnet is a little song
to hold a thing that otherwise cannot
be held: a lonely thing; a death; a bear.

Just the Wind for a Sound, Softly
Carl Phillips

There's a weed whose name I've meant all summer
to find out: in the heat of the day, dangling pods hardly
worth the noticing; in the night, blue flowers . . . It's as if
a side of me that he'd forgotten had forced into the light,
briefly, a side of him that I'd never seen before, and now
I've seen it. It is hard to see anyone who has become
like your own body to you. And now I can't forget.

To the Woman Crying Uncontrollably in the Next Stall

Kim Addonizio

If you ever woke in your dress at 4 a.m. ever
closed your legs to someone you loved opened
them for someone you didn't moved against
a pillow in the dark stood miserably on a beach
seaweed clinging to your ankles paid
good money for a bad haircut backed away
from a mirror that wanted to kill you bled
into the back seat for lack of a tampon
if you swam across a river under rain sang
using a dildo for a microphone stayed up
to watch the moon eat the sun entire
ripped out the stitches in your heart
because why not if you think nothing &
no one can / listen I love you joy is coming

Phases of the Moon /
Things I Have Done

Ella Frears

New Moon:	I ransacked the house for something that does not exist.
Waxing Crescent:	I ate twelve peaches.
First Quarter:	I Tipp-Exed an old letter from him, leaving only the word *basement*.
Waxing Gibbous:	I put on my favourite underwear and cried in the mirror.
Full Moon:	I buried a pork-chop in the garden, walked backwards, howled.
Waning Gibbous:	I thought a great deal about drilling a hole in my head.
Third Quarter:	I told the neighbour my heart beats only for her.
Waning Crescent:	I stood outside facing the house, waited for myself to appear.

Starlings

Maggie Smith

The starlings choose one piece of sky above the river
    & pour themselves in. They must be a thousand arrows
        pointing in unison one way, then another. That bit of blue
    doesn't belong to them, and they don't belong to the sky,
or to the earth, or to us. Isn't that what you've been taught—
nothing is ours? Haven't you learned to keep the loosest
        possible hold? The small portion of sky boils with birds.
    Near the river's edge, one birch has a knot so much
like an eye, you think it sees you. But of course it doesn't.

Sunday

Primus St. John

Today,
The sea has its own religion;
It is as blue
As an acori bead
I rubbed in my hand.

I think
Of swimming out
    for miles
        and miles
            in prayer.

I think
Of never struggling back
In doubt.

As though
In a world like this
Love starts over and over again.

AUTUMN

The Responsibility of Love

G. E. Patterson

Where you are now, the only lights are stars
and oil lamps flaring on vine-covered porches.
Where you are now, it must be midnight.
No one has bothered to name all the roads
that overlook the sea. The freshened air
smells of myrtle and white jasmine. A church
stands on the headland, and I hope it might
keep one thought of me alive in your head.

Autumn is here: warm days becoming cold.
The trees drop more leaves, love, each time it rains.
I eat my meals with the TV turned on,
but softly so the neighbors won't complain.
The kilim is stained by the food I spilled
the first day, and the second, you were gone.

Against Nostalgia

Ada Limón

If I had known, back then, you were coming,
when I first thought love could be the thing
to save me after all, if I had known, would I
have still glued myself to the back of his
motorcycle while we flew across the starless
bridge over the East River to where I grew
my first garden behind the wire fencing,
in the concrete raised beds lined by ruby
twilight roses? If I had known it would be you,

who even then I liked to look at, across a room,
always listening rigorously, a self-questioning look,
the way your mouth was always your mouth,
would I have climbed back on that bike again
and again until even I was sick with fumes
and the sticky seat too hot in the early fall?
If I had known, would I have still made mistake
after mistake until I had only the trunk of me
left, stripped and nearly bare of leaves myself?
If I had known, the truth is, I would have kneeled
and said, *Sooner, come to me sooner.*

Going Home
Mark Nepo

It was the middle of the day.
Early September. Light skirting
from under the leaves. I was taking
the compost to the edge of the yard
when I saw you pinching a pot on
the old bench near the birdbath
we'd lugged from Albany. Mira was
lying in the grass, sun closing her
eyes. Something in the quiet light
made me realize that we were now,
in this moment, all we'd hoped for.
I put the can down and sat next to
you. Watched your hands shape
the clay. I wanted to run my fingers
through your hair. A small cloud
bowed and the sun warmed my
hand on your knee.

When You Go

Edwin Morgan

When you go,
if you go,
and I should want to die,
there's nothing I'd be saved by
more than the time
you fell asleep in my arms
in a trust so gentle
I let the darkening room
drink up the evening, till
rest, or the new rain
lightly roused you awake.
I asked if you heard the rain in your dream
and half dreaming still you only said, I love you.

This Morning
Hannah Bonner

Wind devours me like a whole life
left open.
Space, allowance, stars—
everything I'll take.

Why Did It

William J. Harris

Why did it
take all
day
to get nothing
accomplished

Why, I could
have started
at noon
& saved a lot
of time

Passage

Victoria Chang

Every leaf that falls
never stops falling. I once
thought that leaves were leaves.
Now I think they are feeling,
in search of a place—
someone's hair, a park bench, a
finger. Isn't that
like us, going from place to
place, looking to be alive?

A leaf, a shadow-hand

Jean Valentine

A leaf, a shadow-hand
blows over my head
from outside time
now & then
this time of year, September

—this happens—
—it's well known—
a soul locked away inside
not knowing anyone,
walking around, but inside:

I was like this once,
and you, whose shadow-hand
(kindness) just now blew over my head, again,
you said, "Don't ever think you're a monster."

On Friendship

Henri Cole

Lately, remembering anything involves an ability
to forget something else. Watching the news,
I writhe and moan; my mind is not itself.
Lying next to a begonia from which black ants come and go,
I drink a vodka. Night falls. This seems a balm
for wounds that are not visible in the gaudy daylight.
Sometimes, a friend cooks dinner; our lives commingle.
In loneliness, I fear me, but in society I'm like a soldier
kneeling on soft mats. Everything seems possible,
as when I hear birds that awaken at 4 a.m. or see
a veil upon a face. Beware the heart is lean red meat.
The mind feeds on this. I carry on my shoulder
a bow and arrow for protection. I believe whatever
I do next will surpass what I have done.

Text

Carol Ann Duffy

I tend the mobile now
like an injured bird.

We text, text, text
our significant words.

I re-read your first,
your second, your third,

look for your small *xx*,
feeling absurd.

The codes we send
arrive with a broken chord.

I try to picture your hands,
their image is blurred.

Nothing my thumbs press
will ever be heard.

[As I Dig for Wild Orchids]

Izumi Shikibu

As I dig for wild orchids
in the autumn fields,
it is the deeply-bedded root
that I desire,
not the flower.

Translated by Jane Hirshfield
with Mariko Aratani

To a Daughter Leaving Home

Linda Pastan

When I taught you
at eight to ride
a bicycle, loping along
beside you
as you wobbled away
on two round wheels,
my own mouth rounding
in surprise when you pulled
ahead down the curved
path of the park,
I kept waiting
for the thud
of your crash as I
sprinted to catch up,
while you grew
smaller, more breakable
with distance,
pumping, pumping
for your life, screaming
with laughter,
the hair flapping
behind you like a
handkerchief waving
goodbye.

Flowers

Jay Bernard

Will anybody speak of this
the way the flowers do,
the way the common speaks
of the fearless dying leaves?

Will anybody speak of this
the way the common does,
the way the fearless dying leaves
speak of the coming cold?

Will anybody speak of this
the way the fearless dying leaves
speak of the coming cold
and the quiet it will bring?

Will anybody speak of this
the coming of the cold,
the quiet it will bring,
the fire we beheld?

Will anybody speak of this
the quiet it will bring
the fire we beheld,
the garlands at the gate?

Will anybody speak of this
the fire we beheld
the garlands at the gate
the way the flowers do?

A Drunken Phone Call

Nikki Giovanni

A drunken phone call
From a middle-aged woman
In the middle of the night
After *SportsCenter*
Reminds me
That life is short
And cold
And mean
And maybe I should
Have called you
Like I said
I would

The Wind Did What
the Wind Came to Do

Luther Hughes

You've seen the tired ceremony of felled trees.
You've seen the finches toss their dignity aside
for the hollow mouth at evening's edge,
and the humble Earth saying, *Here, have the night,*
do with it what you please. The perfect moment of love.
Though, it wasn't love. There were bowed trees.
The black clouds galloping across the sky. The wind
moving as if the definition of hunger, going and going
out of habit, nesting as we do when reaching a familiar field,
the natural gust of the body responding to what it finds filling,
resting in the chore of passion. What if this were love,
if wind bargained for beauty, let go of its kingdom?
It must have a thirst for tenderness, stillness in the heart.
Oh surely the distance is closing ever so slightly.
Stay inside me until the storm dies down.

I love you to the moon &

Chen Chen

not back, let's not come back, let's go by the speed of
queer zest & stay up
there & get ourselves a little
moon cottage (so pretty), then start a moon garden

with lots of moon veggies (so healthy), i mean
i was already moonlighting
as an online moonologist
most weekends, so this is the immensely

logical next step, are you
packing your bags yet, don't forget your
sailor moon jean jacket, let's wear
our sailor moon jean jackets while twirling in that lighter,

queerer moon gravity, let's love each other
(so good) on the moon, let's love
the moon
on the moon

Everything Is Dying, Nothing Is Dead
Saeed Jones

It's a bright October morning
inside my annihilation

                and that song, the one hooked
in my ear like an heirloom loop, nears

the verse that always obliterates me
back into innocence

                        while he hums
in the shower, rinsing last night

into the drain, as I rise to open a window
only to realize

                he's opened one for me already:

the autumn air has always been here,
lacing our every breath

        and I love the man who knows I love
the sweet-smoke smell of approaching death.

My Beloved Finds Me
Everywhere but Here

Rio Cortez

We are both poets
so I ask you
to write me into a poem
and you say: here, this one
is about shaping you
into a wave
or here
you are a horse
with lace reins
and I look
finding only music
or what could be
your mother so
I ask again *where am I*
and you say: who else
could I mean
when I write: sweet
witch, write: teeth you
say: can't you see it turn
like you do

Fall Song

Joy Harjo

It is a dark fall day.
The earth is slightly damp with rain.
I hear a jay.
The cry is blue.
I have found you in the story again.
Is there another word for "divine"?
I need a song that will keep sky open in my mind.
If I think behind me, I might break.
If I think forward, I lose now.
Forever will be a day like this
Strung perfectly on the necklace of days.
Slightly overcast
Yellow leaves
Your jacket hanging in the hallway
Next to mine.

Song of the Night Worker

Jessica Traynor

The rain on the bus window
breaks the city into splinters.
Which one of them is hiding you?

I'm pulling the night with me,
let it slip from your shoulders,
see it snag the stars along its hem.

I'm tossing the dawn to you—
cup its flame in your palms
feed it your soft breath

fan it back to me across the miles,
so I can look up, where I am,
at the sky we share.

Fall

Ursula K. Le Guin

O No
vember
held gold
past ember
last flash
kestrel over
amber red gash rust
to bare
endure and somber
clear
yes

If You Aren't Busy
I Think I'm on Fire

Wendy Xu

I worry that someone is right about the end of the world.
If we performed an elaborate ritual
to prevent it, who could say we didn't succeed? The deer live
on to cause another traffic jam, white tails flaring
in the sun. There is no way to disprove
you are infinite. I walk into a yellow house and a calendar
says 1973, the ceilings drag wires from room
to empty room. If we ordered the total annihilation of other people,
would we still need other people? Sunlight coming down
like a yellow tambourine of leaves.

Ode to My Homegirls

Safia Elhillo

smelling of orange rind   of cardamom
   most beautiful girls in the world   *wake up bitch*
    we're getting waffles   *you can keep crying*

but you're going out   my marriages
   my alibis   my bright & hardy stalks
    of protea   & all i know of love i learned

at thirteen   dialing basma's home phone
   by heart   to three-way call whatever boy
    so that weeks later   when the phone bill came

only basma's familiar number beside the time stamp
   clearing my name   basma herself staying awake
    for hours   to hang up the phone after

you who send pictures of your rashes
   to the group text   & long voice notes
    from the bathtub   your laughter echoing against the tiles

you who scatter the world's map   piling into
   cheap buses & budget airlines   four of us asleep
    in my dorm bed   six of us overflowing

my studio apartment   false lashes for weeks after
   like commas in my every pillowcase   you clog my toilet
    & admit it   you text me screenshots

from the gucci fashion show   *getting rich*
   so i can get u this   & when i lived alone
      & that man followed me

one night home from the six train
   up lexington   & into the hallway
      tried for hours to break open my front door

you took turns from all your cities   & stayed
   overnight with me on the phone   for three days
      snoring & murmuring in your sleep

What Came to Me

Jane Kenyon

I took the last
dusty piece of china
out of the barrel.
It was your gravy boat,
with a hard, brown
drop of gravy still
on the porcelain lip.
I grieved for you then
as I never had before.

Dream with Horse

Aria Aber

Already, November makes a fool of me—
sun secretes its tacky, yellow gauze on what
the snowmelt has divided. Slaughterhouse.
The domesticated nag. I am at a loss in the shadow

of the spruces. I freeze. A faint scent of equine.
Taut as a tuning fork, I meditate on the horse's
heavy meat, its nostrils glistening like a liver,
laboring to breathe. The real shackle, of course,

isn't my flesh, but my mind's harness committing
its slow violence through my eyes. Looking for
a sign, I smear on snow my sputum, then hair.
Not a day passes that I pass as belonging here.

[We Mention the Cat]

CAConrad

we mention the
cat aging in place
of the obvious but
it wasn't like that
we are not afraid
of growing old so
long as we know
love each day
what has happened to you
writing a poem about love
what has happened to any
of us for thinking we
can possibly
survive
even
reasonably
without
it
because
nothing
keeps
me wanting life like love

New York, November

J. Mae Barizo

Today, my restless, yellow leaves
are thrashing through the wind.
The air in this city is thick
with fear and want and every
day the men and women
start to build again. Our lives
as we keep track of them
are acted out in simple
gestures: hand to mouth,
a gasp, clear-cut kiss
or not. Nothing harmful
nothing said. The things
we never speak of are like
the lost debris or yellow leaves
in any city, any fall. But
something tells us this
is different. Maybe it's
that sad, burnt scent
without a name. Perhaps
it's just New York, miles
from where you are.
All I can really be sure
of these days are the words
I write you from my crowded
heart, and the yellow leaves
and the way one season
meets the next, violently.

Sleeping with You

Ellen Bass

Is there anything more wonderful?
After we have floundered
through our separate pain

we come to this. I bind myself to you,
like otters wrapped in kelp, so the current
will not steal us as we sleep.

Through the night we turn together,
rocked in the shallow surf,
pebbles polished by the sea.

Thank You

Ross Gay

If you find yourself half naked
and barefoot in the frosty grass, hearing,
again, the earth's great, sonorous moan that says
you are the air of the now and gone, that says
all you love will turn to dust,
and will meet you there, do not
raise your fist. Do not raise
your small voice against it. And do not
take cover. Instead, curl your toes
into the grass, watch the cloud
ascending from your lips. Walk
through the garden's dormant splendor.
Say only, thank you.
Thank you.

WINTER

Lake Zürich

Charif Shanahan

When I arrived in evening you
drank coffee by the fireplace

ashless in winter: I knew

what slant of myself
would keep you.

At the abandoned boathouse

remnants of a party: you
placed your hand

where you knew I hurt;

I kicked a cup and leaned
into your weight.

Wake Up

Noelle Kocot

Tumbling at the edge
Of disaster,

This is how I lived.
Oh see how the chrysanthemums

Are dry now,
Yet still beautiful.

Poem with Evening Coming On

C. D. Wright

a dog has appeared at the gate
for the second day in a row
against a dirty peach sky
a single car wobbles into the sun

The Voice in My Head
Speaks English Now

José Olivarez

snow finds me underneath layers. maybe
the cold wants to hang out. take me skiing.
wants me to see winter isn't a bad country
& it's not, but i'm still shivering. i make snow
angels & come out snot-nosed. throat blistering.

it never stops being cold. my new voice fit
with coughing. my friends say summer is coming.
they're lying. on gray days, i wear the sun, but
it falls off my shoulders. if you catch my mom
in good light, it's impossible to tell where the sun ends.

i tell myself that's where i'm from, but i'm not
sure. when i was a baby i used to get fevers.
maybe that's why my parents planted me in snow.
now i'm a long way from the fire my parents feared
& so close to this new blue flame.

Dear—

Donika Kelly

I take the first snowfall for ash. Mistake,
I mean, the first flake that comes wisping
down for the remnant of some thing burned,
perhaps, for warmth or in error. When we were
young, we stood with our backs not to the past
or future but toward the hot desperation
of being alive and for right now.
At the canyon's edge, the wind, thick as a hand,
readied to push you into gorge and river
rock. *Come back*, I said. And the wind took
my voice too. Love, there is no fire here—
only water, finally, drifting
to coat the grass, to keep it green, to heap
the limbs and needles in wet, heavy white.

i'm going back to Minnesota
where sadness makes sense

Danez Smith

o California, don't you know the sun is only a god
if you learn to starve for her? i'm over the ocean

i stood at its lip, dressed in down, praying for snow.
i know i'm strange, too much light makes me nervous

at least in this land where the trees always bear green.
i know something that doesn't die can't be beautiful.

have you ever stood on a frozen lake, California?
the sun above you, the snow & stalled sea—a field of mirror

all demanding to be the sun, everything around you
is light & it's gorgeous & if you stay too long it will kill you.

it's so sad, you know? you're the only warm thing for miles
the only thing that can't shine.

There You Are

Victoria Adukwei Bulley

There you are
this cold day
boiling the water on the stove
pouring the herbs into the pot
hawthorn, rose;
buying the tulips
& looking at them, holding
your heart in your hands at the table
saying *please, please*, to nobody else
here in the kitchen with you.
How hard, how heavy this all is.
How beautiful, these things you do,
in case they help, these things you do
which, although you haven't said it yet,
say that you want to live.

Perfect Song

Heather Christle

I remember walking through the morning
after a night of heavy snow and drink
with headphones on and they played
me the most perfect song: no one
was awake and I was hungover
young as clean as a piano
I thought and at any moment
someone might fall in love with me I was
that woven into the electric
cold bright air and for weeks
after I went through the album
in search of the song but could not
find it and later much later I saw
that what I had taken to be the song
was in fact the joyous concordance of
a moment that would not come again

These Days

Charles Olson

whatever you have to say, leave
the roots on, let them
dangle

And the dirt

       Just to make clear
       where they came from

[*I won't be able to write from the grave*]

Fanny Howe

I won't be able to write from the grave
so let me tell you what I love:
oil, vinegar, salt, lettuce, brown bread, butter,
cheese and wine, a windy day, a fireplace,
the children nearby, poems and songs,
a friend sleeping in my bed—

and the short northern nights.

Miss You. Would Love to Take a Walk with You

Gabrielle Calvocoressi

Do not care if you just arrive in your skeleton.
Would love to take a walk with you. Miss you.
Would love to make you shrimp saganaki.
Like you used to make me when you were alive.
Love to feed you. Sit over steaming
bowls of pilaf. Little roasted tomatoes
covered in pepper and nutmeg. Miss you.
Would love to walk to the post office with you.
Bring the ghost dog. We'll walk past the waterfall
and you can tell me about the after.
Wish you. Wish you would come back for a while.
Don't even need to bring your skin sack. I'll know
you. I know you will know me even though. I'm
bigger now. Grayer. I'll show you my garden.
I'd like to hop in the leaf pile you raked but if you
want to jump in? I'll rake it for you. Miss you
standing looking out at the river with your rake
in your hand. Miss you in your puffy blue jacket.
They're hip now. I can bring you a new one
if you'll only come by. Know I told you
it was okay to go. Know I told you
it was okay to leave me. Why'd you believe me?
You always believed me. Wish you would
come back so we could talk about truth.
Miss you. Wish you would walk through my
door. Stare out from the mirror. Come through
the pipes.

Watching My Friend Pretend Her Heart Is Not Breaking

Rosemerry Wahtola Trommer

On Earth, just a teaspoon of neutron star
would weigh six billion tons. Six billion tons
equals the collective weight of every animal
on earth. Including the insects. Times three.

Six billion tons sounds impossible
until I consider how it is to swallow grief—
just a teaspoon and one might as well have consumed
a neutron star. How dense it is,
how it carries inside it the memory of collapse.
How difficult it is to move then.
How impossible to believe that anything
could lift that weight.

There are many reasons to treat each other
with great tenderness. One is
the sheer miracle that we are here together
on a planet surrounded by dying stars.
One is that we cannot see what
anyone else has swallowed.

Self-Care

Solmaz Sharif

Have you tried
rose hydrosol? Smoky quartz
in a steel bottle

of glacial water? Tincture
drawn from the stamens
of daylilies grown
on the western sides

of two-story homes?
Pancreas of toad?
Deodorant paste?

Have you removed
your metal fillings? Made peace
with your mother? With all
the mothers you can? Or tried

car exhaust? Holding your face
to the steaming kettle?
Primal screamed into

a down-alternative pillow
in a wood while tree-bathing?
Have you finally stopped
shoulding all over yourself?

Has your copay increased?
Right hip stiffened?
Has the shore risen

as you closed up the shop?
And have you put your weight
behind its glass door to keep
the ocean out? All of it?

Rang the singing bowl
next to the sloping toilet?
Mainlined lithium?

Colored in another mandala?
Have you looked
yourself in the mirror
and found the blessed halo

of a ring light in each iris?
Have you been content enough
being this content? Whose

shop was it?

Author's Prayer

Ilya Kaminsky

If I speak for the dead, I must leave
this animal of my body,

I must write the same poem over and over,
for an empty page is the white flag of their surrender.

If I speak for them, I must walk on the edge
of myself, I must live as a blind man

who runs through rooms without
touching the furniture.

Yes, I live. I can cross the streets asking "What year is it?"
I can dance in my sleep and laugh

in front of the mirror.
Even sleep is a prayer, Lord,

I will praise your madness, and
in a language not mine, speak

of music that wakes us, music
in which we move. For whatever I say

is a kind of petition, and the darkest
days must I praise.

I still have everything you gave me

Naomi Shihab Nye

It is dusty on the edges.

Slightly rotten.

I guard it without thinking.

Focus on it once a year
when I shake it out in the wind.

I do not ache.

I would not trade.

Elegy VIII (Missing you)

Jason Schneiderman

I thought I'd find you here, that I'd finish these poems
and you would stand out as clear as the day. As bright
as the moon. I hate those poets who tell you that
they love, but never make clear whom they love.
My mother's eyes are nothing like the sun. How do I
miss my mother? Let me count the ways. So where
are you? I couldn't believe you let yourself
be filmed for the video they showed at your tribute,
and I wanted to tell everyone, *That's only her voice
when she's nervous. That's only her face when she
has to be on display and she doesn't like it.* But at least
you were there. Everyone knows you can't write
your way out of grief. Everyone knows that grief
never turns into anything but grief, and OK, I can grieve
you forever. But I wanted you here, in the middle
of my book. Not a complaint about what I lost
or what it feels like to lose it. But you. Your smile.
Your denim dress.

The Years

Alex Dimitrov

All the parties you spent
watching the room
from a balcony
where someone joined you
to smoke then returned.
And how it turns out no one
had the childhood they wanted,
and how they'd tell you this
a little drunk, a little slant
in less time than it took
to finish a cigarette
because sad things
can't be explained.
Behind the glass and inside,
all your friends buzzed.
You could feel the shape
of their voices. You could
tell from their eyes they were
in some other place. 1999
or 2008 or last June.
Of course, it's important
to go to parties. To make
life a dress or a drink
or suede shoes someone wears
in the rain. On the way home,
in the car back, the night sky

played its old tricks. The stars
arranged themselves quietly.
The person you thought of drove
under them. Away from the party,
(just like you) into the years.

I Am Filled with Love

Anna Świrszczyńska

I am filled with love
as a great tree with the wind,
as a sponge with the ocean,
as a great life with suffering,
as time with death.

What is now will soon be past

Yrsa Daley-Ward

Just because you do it
doesn't mean you always will.
Whether you're dancing dust
or breathing light
you're never exactly the same,
twice.

January 7, 1997

Joe Wenderoth

What a joy it is to be alive! To wake late in the morning and have cups and cups and cups of coffee, and in the heightened blind pulse that follows to *play*, to *let language have its way*, to let the business of day *close down* with all of us still inside! We absolutely hang together in how dim the day gets. We hang by sentences. Listen! We hang by the sound of the shadow of a thread!

Winter Honey

June Jordan

Sugar come
and sugar go
Sugar dumb
but sugar know
ain' nothin' run me for my money
nothin' sweet like winter honey

Sugar high
and sugar low
Sugar pie
and sugar dough
Then sugar throw
a sugar fit
And sugar find
a sugar tit
But never mind
what sugar find
ain' nothin' run me for my money
nothin' sweet like winter honey

Sugar come
and please don' go
Sugar dumb
but oh-my: Oh!
Ain' nothin' run me for my money
nothin' sweet like winter honey

To the Winter Apricot Blossom

Emily Jungmin Yoon

Did I trick you,
with the glow from my window,
the warmth of my skin?

It started with a lone flower,
ember-like in the lifting dusk,
burgeoning on the branch

nosing into my room.
At night the floret shadow dropped
onto my page, my arm, my poem.

In the snow you were heavy
with a hundred bulbs
to light the winter into spring.

A cold misty morning.
You alone illuminate the sky,
small lanterns, red, bursting lobes.

On a Train

Wendy Cope

The book I've been reading
rests on my knee. You sleep.

It's beautiful out there—
fields, little lakes and winter trees
in February sunlight,
every car park a shining mosaic.

Long, radiant minutes,
your hand in my hand,
still warm, still warm.

Maybe in Another Life

Tiana Clark

I think of the kids I may or may not have. I think about
their hair, the possible dark-brown curls. Baby fingers
tapping on my face. I haven't made up my mind yet,
but my body is making decisions before I am ready

to make them. I can't seem to say what it is I want
out loud. I can almost see all my different lives, almost
taste them, like trying to catch the tail end of a cinematic
dream before it evaporates. I want to capture it, a glimpse,

sneak a peek at each distant future before the View-Master
reel clicks. I want to follow the perfume of each life
I could live and linger in it: the vanillas. Milk leaking
from my breasts. Cereal. The piquant odor of parenthood.

The one where I am a mother negotiating happiness.
The one where I am not a mother and still negotiating
happiness, beauty, and rest. Almost 39, and I've never
loved myself more, yet nostalgia wavers all around me

like a montage of mirages muddling memories, complicating
hope, making me miss things I've already mourned.
The bargaining—ain't it a bitch? The bargaining aspect
of grief, to constantly release that which I've already

let go of, but how the water in my mind brings it all back
like the flood current each day, and each morning, in the ebb
I see the seafloor for what it is, another landscape of loss
and renewal, another augur deciphering the tea leaves

in the tide pool revealing the children I might never name, have, or hold. There is a finite number of eggs and books inside me. I am trying to release them. I am trying to mourn the possible futures bursting before me in a fantastic finale

of fireworks, bursting in my mouth like red caviar as I try to find the right words to say goodbye to little faces I can only imagine. I'm not sure what I want. Each decision seems to dissolve at the edge of the beach softened by the watercolor

cream of winter floating above the same shore where Eliot wrote "The Waste Land" after a mental breakdown a hundred and one years before me, writing "On Margate Sands. / I can connect / Nothing with nothing." I keep looking at the gentle waves

for answers without trying to make another metaphor. What if the image of what I'm feeling is too heavy to be carried over into language? Maybe in another life you get to live out all the lives you've imagined. Maybe in this life

I become who I am by not knowing—

Endings

Sandra Lim

The story has two endings.

It has one ending

and then another.

Do you hear me?

I do not have the heart

to edit the other out.

Morning Love Poem

Tara Skurtu

Dreamt last night I fed you, unknowingly,
something you were allergic to.

And you were gone, like that.

You don't have even a single allergy,
but still. The dream cracked. Cars nose-dived

off snow banks into side streets. Sometimes
dreams slip poison, make the living

dead then alive again, twirling
in an unfamiliar room.

It's hard to say *I need you* enough.

Today I did. Walked into your morning
shower fully clothed. All the moments

we stop ourselves just because we might
feel embarrassed or impractical, or get wet.

Advice

Langston Hughes

Folks, I'm telling you,
birthing is hard
and dying is mean—
so get yourself
a little loving
in between.

To Know the Dark

Wendell Berry

To go in the dark with a light is to know the light.
To know the dark, go dark. Go without sight,
and find that the dark, too, blooms and sings,
and is traveled by dark feet and dark wings.

Letter to a Moon Child

Michael S. Harper

Moon child:
March is coming
In mixed anger,
To an eventual end.
The trees have cracked
Under the weight of ice,
Blotting power lines,
And we have been without light,
Days, nights, together.
Elms are first to bloom
Slowly, in fear of constant
Virus, that heedless,
Will kill them off in ten years;
This year they bloom.
The spindly trees,
Taking shape, resist
The inlet, hornet,
And salt night air.
In this ribald quiet,
Revisited without shame,
There is evidence,
Ornate, and our hunger.

SPRING

Coping

Audre Lorde

It has rained for five days
running
the world is
a round puddle
of sunless water
where small islands
are only beginning
to cope
a young boy
in my garden
is bailing out water
from his flower patch
when I ask him why
he tells me
young seeds that have not seen sun
forget
and drown easily.

[I want to wake up]

Bhanu Kapil

I want to wake up
In the arms of the person
I love
And drink coffee with them
On a balcony
That opens up to a forest
Where the moss
Glows green
In the pouring rain.
We are both
Poets
Or one of us is.
It doesn't matter to me
What this person does
For a living
Or who they are
Inside gender's
Hall.
Light a candle, beloved,
And lay me down
On the forest floor.
Am I your queen?

As for What the Rain Can Do

D. A. Powell

wash me in blossoms yet to come
lift my boat

flood the rice fields where the egret lands
complex math

rinse off a bench
turn on a dime

give you something to think about
feed an aspiring stream

tell you by thunder it's coming
stand you up

play a little music on the rooftop
get a body good and wet

open the golden tulips
mix us a drink

I Could Let You Go

Thomas Dooley

as if opening a crepe sail
on a raft of linden
downriver with no
glacial cut swerve down
soft like bourbon if I could
ask the waters then
to chop to shake
an apology when you cry
I feel a wet bank in me
ring dry here I'll wrap you
in the piano shawl from the upright
to your fists a spray
of dandelion and comb my last
compassion to grasp.
Goodbye, friend. Willows
dip to your lips
dew from their leafed
digits feast now
on the cold blue soup
of sky the iron from bankwater
gilts your blood I'll break
a bottle on your gunwale
and read broken
poems from the shore
as the dark river
curls back white from the cheap timber
as if letting what's made to drift
drift.

Why Bother?
Sean Thomas Dougherty

Because right now, there is   someone

out there with

a wound   in the exact shape

                                      of your words.

I Need a Poem

Kyla Jamieson

Can we talk about the moon
tonight? Low & full
in the baby-blue sky. A friend
at my door, the sound
of her laugh & well-loved
heart. I want to be held
up like that. I need a poem
about happiness I haven't
written yet, an ode
to the ducks in my neighbours'
pool, another for the pink
magnolias of spring—some trees
make it look so easy: *Yes*
I can hold all this beauty up.

Myth

Ata Moharreri

Each tree is in love
with one star.

Their tears come to life
as fireflies.

We sometimes feel them
burning our eyes.

3 O'clock in the Morning

Jasmine Mans

You call,
at three in the morning.

I answer,
we are the only two,
in the world,
awake.

We talk,
like we discovered God
before everyone else
did.

Romance

Timothy Liu

His body wasn't terribly abused.

More like a copy of a used book
bought online with very minimal

marginalia scrawled in pencil

by its previous owner who lost
interest after the first few pages—

something one can easily erase.

[You]

Jos Charles

You
touch long
irretrievable
beside you again
  me again
in the dark of our certainty
I hold like a stone &
even you I turn
my head to a thousand possible things
gone It is all I hold
now & spring

A Cedary Fragrance

Jane Hirshfield

Even now,
decades after,
I wash my face with cold water—

Not for discipline,
nor memory,
nor the icy, awakening slap,

but to practice
choosing
to make the unwanted wanted.

I Am the Horse

Dorothea Lasky

I am the horse people should bet on
I am the person who will likely save you from a fire
I am the person who is black smoke
And blows black smoke in your eyes
I am the squeaky noise at night
I am the tables, and paper, and slugs
I am the thing that most excites you
I am the thing that most excites you
I am the horse that you should bet on
When you put your money down

Praising Spring

Linda Gregg

The day is taken by each thing and grows complete.
I go out and come in and go out again,
confused by a beauty that knows nothing of delay,
rushing like fire. All things move faster
than time and make a stillness thereby. My mind
leans back and smiles, having nothing to say.
Even at night I go out with a light and look
at the growing. I kneel and look at one thing
at a time. A white spider on a peony bud.
I have nothing to give, and make a poor servant,
but I can praise the spring. Praise this wildness
that does not heed the hour. The doe that does not
stop at dark but continues to grow all night long.
The beauty in every degree of flourishing. Violets
lift to the rain and the brook gets louder than ever.
The old German farmer is asleep and the flowers go on
opening. There are stars. Mint grows high. Leaves
bend in the sunlight as the rain continues to fall.

What She Might Pray

Moyra Donaldson

No matter how far I have drifted,
even if land is nowhere to be seen,
do not let the sea completely own me.
I could not bear to hear no other rhythm
but the tide's relentlessness.
Do not abandon me. Anchor me with love.

Truth is I would like to escape myself

Nour Al Ghraowi

Truth is I would like to escape myself.
            Detach my body from my skin,
peel it layer by layer to uncover
            beneath the surface of petals
and thorns piled up year after year,
            who I am and who I want to be.
I want to be the flower that grows
            in dirt, the feather that flies free between
the cracks of fences. A wise woman
            once told me, *don't worry about you,*
worry about who you could be.
            I want to be the woman who sits
on a desk and writes pieces of oceans,
            rivers on a white space in a place
where imagination has no border.

Splendor
Cole Krawitz

in a blossom

       a knowing, a clarity

to fall and burst

and bud and burst

       to temper the sunlight's solidity—

petals, ceremonious, holy, as if

maybe, a song, or the high note

       a diva hits

her arms outstretched

       waking up the light

Miracles

Brenda Shaughnessy

I spent the whole day
crying and writing, until
they became the same,

as when the planet covers the sun
with all its might and still
I can see it, or when one dead

body gives its heart
to a name on a list. A match.
A light. Sailing a signal

flare behind me for another to find.
A scratch on the page
is a supernatural act, one twisting

fire out of water, blood out of stone.
We can read us. We are not alone.

Orchard

Andrea Cohen

The apple trees
were growing

peaches, and
in the lemon

grove, persimmons.
I'd have saved

a plum
from the fig

tree—but
I dreamed you.

The Poem

Franz Wright

It was like getting a love letter from a tree

Eyes closed forever to find you—

There *is* a life which
if I could have it
I would have chosen for myself from the beginning

Travelling Together

W. S. Merwin

If we are separated I will
try to wait for you
on your side of things

your side of the wall and the water
and of the light moving at its own speed
even on leaves that we have seen
I will wait on one side

while a side is there

How to Not Be a Perfectionist
Molly Brodak

People are vivid
and small
and don't live
very long—

Checkout

Caroline Bird

I think "so, this is death" and wonder why
I can still see through my eyes. An angel
approaches with a feedback form asking
how I'd rate my life (very good, good,
average, bad, very bad) and I intend to tick
"average" followed by a rant then I recall
your face like a cartoon treasure chest
glowing with gold light, tick "very good,"
and in the comment box below I write
"nice job." The angel asks if I enjoyed
my stay and I say "Oh yes, I'd definitely
come again" and he gives me a soft look
meaning "that won't be possible but thanks
all the same," clicks his pen and vanishes.

Fluent

John O'Donohue

I would love to live
Like a river flows,
Carried by the surprise
Of its own unfolding.

Meditations in an Emergency

Cameron Awkward-Rich

I wake up & it breaks my heart. I draw the blinds
& the thrill of rain breaks my heart. I go outside.
I ride the train, walk among the buildings, men in
Monday suits. The flight of doves, the city of tents
beneath the underpass, the huddled mass, old
women hawking roses, & children all of them,
break my heart. There's a dream I have in which I
love the world. I run from end to end like fingers
through her hair. There are no borders, only wind.
Like you, I was born. Like you, I was raised in the
institution of dreaming. Hand on my heart. Hand
on my stupid heart.

Don't Be Afraid

Alicia Ostriker

This is when I want to open you
Like a sweater, like a jacket

That you have kept closed,
To walk into your heart

As if it were a major avenue
In an unpolluted city, and I could hike

From one end of the city to the other
With all I own on my back,

Breathing the fresh
Air of your heart, looking at clouds and buildings.

No Romance

Jacqueline Suskin

No one ever shows up
at my door dancing,
with poems pouring out.
A note written at the airport,
an album of perfect songs,
a brass ring with colored glass.
I want more, but not in a foolish way.
I want an in-sync, energetic wave.
Show me you were thinking of me
when I wasn't there. Allow me
to witness myself
as the never-ending source of inspiration
that fills your silly body
with something
that makes each breath better.

Scarf

Rita Dove

Whoever claims beauty
lies in the eye
of the beholder

has forgotten the music
silk makes settling
across a bared

neck: skin never touched
so gently except
by a child

or a lover.

We Love What We Have

Mosab Abu Toha

We love what we have, no matter how little,
because if we don't, everything will be gone. If we don't,
we will no longer exist, since there will be nothing here for us.
What's here is something that we are still
building. It's something we cannot yet see,
because we are part
of it.
Someday soon, this building will stand on its own, while we,
we will be the trees that protect it from the fierce
wind, the trees that will give shade
to children sleeping inside or playing on swings.

[from *For M*]

Mikko Harvey

The number
of hours
we have
together is
actually not
so large.
Please linger
near the
door uncomfortably
instead of
just leaving.
Please forget
your scarf
in my
life and
come back
later for
it.

[To be alive]

Gregory Orr

To be alive: not just the carcass
But the spark.
That's crudely put, but . . .

If we're not supposed to dance,
Why all this music?

ACKNOWLEDGMENTS

Many thanks to all the readers on Instagram whose support and community keeps the page going. It is an honor to be able to share poetry with you. I am grateful for people like Noah Falck, Lindsay Miller, Jordan Karnes, Thomas Dooley, Mara Scanlon, and Elizabeth Metzger, who early on saw my work and encouraged me to continue and grow as a curator.

Thank you, Jessica Wallenfels, Rich Gabe, Elsa Muñoz, Alexander Chee, Valerie June, Jonathan Wells, James Richardson, José Olivarez, J. Mae Barizo, Mark Mallman, Rachel Lauren Myers, Namita Wiggers, Andy Wakefield, Leah Doolittle, Dee Loeffler, Sarah Peeden, Hannah Bonner, Cari Gray, Christine Clark, Vanessa Naff, Yrsa Daley-Ward, and many more who have supported me through Patreon and beyond. You pull me into the light on the darkest days.

Thank you to Jenny Xu, Ifeoma Anyoku, and the team at Atria, Washington Square Press, and Simon & Schuster UK for taking care with this collection.

This book came to be because of Maggie Cooper: thank you for seeing and guiding my potential.

Infinite love to my ma and pop for filling my life with all the best words. I find you in these poems; I find you everywhere.

My heart is full with love and gratitude for my friends, my chosen family, including Agnes who always guides my words. For Stephanie, Michael, Laurie, and Kevin, thank you. Especially grateful for Jessie, Renée, Sam, and Adam who allow me to read all the poems aloud and ask "which one?" Often without you my indecision would take over.

To my partner: thank you for being my eyes, keeping me full, for your patience and sweetness that fill home with love.

Thank you to all the book lovers who fill their shelves with poetry, who gift poems to their friends and family: you keep print alive.

To all the poets, I am forever grateful for all you give; your words are part of me.

CREDITS

SUMMER

Li-Young Lee, "One Heart" from *Book of My Nights.* Copyright © 2001 by Li-Young Lee. Reprinted with the permission of The Permissions Company, LLC on behalf of BOA Editions, Ltd., boaeditions.org.

"/ˈmīgrənt/." Reprinted from *Cleave.* Copyright © 2021 by Tiana Nobile. Used with permission of the publisher, Hub City Press. All rights reserved.

"Idea" from *And Yet* by Kate Baer. Copyright © 2022 by Kate Baer. Used by permission of HarperCollins Publishers.

Ron Padgett, "The Love Cook" from *Collected Poems.* Copyright © 2001 by Ron Padgett. Reprinted with the permission of The Permissions Company, LLC on behalf of Coffee House Press, coffeehousepress.org.

Aja Monet, "The ways of the many" from *My Mother Was a Freedom Fighter.* Copyright © 2017 by Aja Monet. Reprinted with the permission of Haymarket Books.

Franny Choi, "Strawberry Moon" from *Soft Science.* Copyright © 2019 by Franny Choi. Reprinted with the permission of The Permissions Company, LLC on behalf of Alice James Books, alicejamesbooks.org.

Ama Codjoe, "On Seeing and Being Seen" from *Bluest Nude*. Copyright © 2022 by Ama Codjoe. Reprinted with the permission of The Permissions Company, LLC on behalf of Milkweed Editions, milkweed.org.

"Cento for the Night I Said, 'I Love You'" from *Ordinary Beast* by Nicole Sealey. Copyright © 2017 by Nicole Sealey. Used by permission of HarperCollins Publishers.

"I went" from *The Complete Poems of Cavafy* by C. P. Cavafy, translated by Rae Dalven. Copyright © 1948, 1949, 1959, 1961 by Rae Dalven. Used by permission of Harper Collins Publishers.

"Loveable." From *All the Names Given* by Raymond Antrobus © Raymond Antrobus, 2021, published by Tin House, reproduced with kind permission by David Higham Associates.

"Tired of Love Poems." Selections from *I Do Everything I'm Told*. Copyright © 2023 by Megan Fernandes. Reprinted with permission from Tin House Books.

Jenny George, "Tin Bucket" from *After Image.* Copyright © 2024 by Jenny George. Reprinted with the permission of The Permissions Company, LLC on behalf of Copper Canyon Press, coppercanyonpress.org.

Mary Ruefle, "Happiness," from *Dunce.* Copyright © 2020 by Mary Ruefle. Reprinted with the permission of The Permissions Company, LLC on behalf of Wave Books, wavepoetry.com.

"Ode to Hunger" from *O* by Zeina Hashem Beck, copyright © 2022 by Zeina Hashem Beck. Used by permission of Penguin Books, an imprint of Penguin Publishing Group, a division of Penguin Random House LLC. All rights reserved.

"Pattern" from *Lean Against This Late Hour* by Garous Abdolmalekian, translated by Ahmad Nadalizadeh and Idra

Novey, copyright © 2020 by Garous Abdolmalekian. Translation copyright © 2020 by Ahmad Nadalizadeh and Idra Novey. Used by permission of Penguin Books, an imprint of Penguin Publishing Group, a division of Penguin Random House LLC. All rights reserved.

"At a Waterfall, Reykjavik" from *School of Fish* by Eileen Myles, reprinted with permission of Eileen Myles. Copyright © 1997 by Eileen Myles. Courtesy of Black Sparrow Publishers.

"Summer Solstice." Selections from *My Baby First Birthday*. Copyright © 2020 by Jenny Zhang. Reprinted with permission from Tin House Books.

"Think of Others." From *Almond Blossoms and Beyond*, by Mahmoud Darwish, translated by Mohammad Shaheen, published by Interlink Books, an imprint of Interlink Publishing Group, Inc. Reprinted by permission.

Robin Coste Lewis, "43." Originally appeared in *The New Yorker*.

"Jupiter" by Nicholas Hogg, first published in *Missing Person* (Broken Sleep Books, 2023).

Noor Hindi, "Ode" from *Dear God*. Copyright © 2022 by Noor Hindi. Reprinted with the permission of Haymarket Books.

"Tender" by Sophie Klahr. Used by permission of Sophie Klahr.

"Just the Wind for a Sound, Softly" from *Silverchest* by Carl Phillips. Copyright © 2013 by Carl Phillips. Reprinted by permission of Farrar, Straus and Giroux. All Rights Reserved.

"To the Woman Crying Uncontrollably in the Next Stall," from *Now We're Getting Somewhere: Poems* by Kim Addonizio. Copyright © 2021 by Kim Addonizio. Used by permission of W. W. Norton & Company, Inc.

Ella Frears, "Phases of the Moon / Things I Have Done." With permission of the author and publisher. From *Shine, Darling* (Offord Road Books, 2020).

"Starlings." Excerpted from *Goldenrod: Poems* by Maggie Smith. Copyright © 2021 by Maggie Smith. Reprinted with the permission of One Signal Publishers/Atria Books, an Imprint of Simon & Schuster, LLC. All rights reserved.

Primus St. John, "Sunday" from *Communion: New and Selected Poems*. Copyright © 1999 by Primus St. John. Reprinted with the permission of The Permissions Company, LLC on behalf of Copper Canyon Press, copper canyonpress.org.

AUTUMN

G. E. Patterson, "The Responsibility of Love" from *Tug*. Copyright © 1999 by G. E. Patterson. Reprinted with the permission of The Permissions Company, LLC on behalf of Graywolf Press, graywolfpress.org.

Ada Limón, "Against Nostalgia" from *The Hurting Kind: Poems*. Copyright © 2022 by Ada Limón. Reprinted with the permission of The Permissions Company, LLC on behalf of Milkweed Editions, milkweed.org.

"Going Home." Copyright © 2016 by Mark Nepo.

Edwin Morgan, "When You Go" from *Collected Poems*. Copyright © 1985. Used by permission of Carcanet Press.

"This Morning" by Hannah Bonner. From *Another Woman*, Eastover Press, 2024.

Used by permission of Hannah Bonner.

"Why Did It" by William J. Harris. Used by permission of William J. Harris.

Victoria Chang, "Passage" from *Trees Witness Everything*. Copyright © 2022 by Victoria Chang. Reprinted with the permission of The Permissions Company, LLC on behalf of Copper Canyon Press, coppercanyonpress .org.

Jean Valentine, "A leaf, a shadow-hand" from *Shirt in Heaven*. Copyright © 2015 by Jean Valentine. Reprinted with the permission of The Permissions Company, LLC on behalf of Copper Canyon Press, coppercanyonpress.org.

"On Friendship" from *Gravity and Center: Selected Sonnets, 1994–2022* by Henri Cole. Copyright © 2023 by Henri Cole. Reprinted by permission of Farrar, Straus and Giroux. All Rights Reserved.

"Text" from *Rapture* by Carol Ann Duffy. Copyright © 2005 by Carol Ann Duffy. Reprinted by permission of Farrar, Straus and Giroux. All Rights Reserved.

"[As I Dig for Wild Orchids]" by Izumi Shikibu, translated by Jane Hirshfield with Mariko Aratani; from *The Ink Dark Moon: Love Poems by Ono No Komachi and Izumi Shikibu, Women of the Ancient Court of Japan*, translated by Jane Hirshfield with Mariko Aratani, translation copyright © 1986, 1987, 1988, 1989, 1990 by Jane Hirshfield. Used by permission of Vintage Books, an imprint of the Knopf Doubleday Publishing Group, a division of Penguin Random House LLC. All rights reserved.

"To a Daughter Leaving Home." Copyright © 1988 by Linda Pastan, from *Carnival Evening: New and Selected Poems, 1968–1998* by Linda Pastan. Used by permission of W. W. Norton & Company, Inc.

"Flowers." From *Surge* by Jay Bernard published by Chatto & Windus. Copyright © Jay Bernard, 2019. Reprinted by permission of Penguin Books Limited.

"A Drunken Phone Call" from *Bicycles* by Nikki Giovanni. Copyright © 2009 by Nikki Giovanni. Used by permission of HarperCollins Publishers.

Luther Hughes, "The Wind Did What the Wind Came to Do" from *A Shiver in the Leaves*. Copyright © 2022 by Luther Hughes. Reprinted with the permission of The Permissions Company, LLC on behalf of BOA Editions, Ltd., boaeditions.org.

Chen Chen, "I love you to the moon &" from *Explodingly Yours* (Ghost City Press, 2023). Originally published in Poem-a-Day on May 31, 2021, by the Academy of American Poets. Copyright © 2021, 2023 by Chen Chen. Reprinted with the permission of The Permissions Company, LLC on behalf of the poet, chenchenwrites .com.

Saeed Jones, "Everything Is Dying, Nothing Is Dead" from *Alive at the End of the World*. Copyright © 2022 by Saeed Jones. Reprinted with the permission of The Permissions Company, LLC on behalf of Coffee House Press, coffee housepress.org.

"My Beloved Finds Me Everywhere but Here" from *Golden Ax* by Rio Cortez, copyright © 2022 by Rio Cortez. Used by permission of Penguin Books, an imprint of Penguin Publishing Group, a division of Penguin Random House LLC. All rights reserved.

"Fall Song," from *Conflict and Resolution for Holy Beings: Poems* by Joy Harjo. Copyright © 2015 by Joy Harjo. Used by permission of W. W. Norton & Company, Inc.

"Song of the Night Worker" (Part V of "An Island Sings") by Jessica Traynor, *Pit Lullabies* (Bloodaxe Books, 2022). Reproduced with permission of Bloodaxe Books.

"Fall." Copyright © 1999 by Ursula K. Le Guin. First appeared in *Sixty Odd*, published by Shambhala Press in 1999. Reprinted by permission of Ginger Clark Literary, LLC.

Wendy Xu, "If You Aren't Busy I Think I'm on Fire" from *You Are Not Dead*. Copyright © 2013 by Wendy Xu. Reprinted with the permission of The Permissions Company, LLC on behalf of the Cleveland State University Poetry Center, csupoetrycenter.com.

"Ode to My Homegirls" from *Girls That Never Die* by Safia Elhillo, copyright © 2022 by Safia Elhillo. Used by permission of One World, an imprint of Random House, a division of Penguin Random House LLC. All rights reserved.

Jane Kenyon, "What Came to Me" from *Collected Poems*. Copyright © 2005 by The Estate of Jane Kenyon. Reprinted with the permission of The Permissions Company, LLC on behalf of Graywolf Press, graywolfpress.org.

"Dream with Horse." Reprinted from *Hard Damage* by Aria Aber by permission of the University of Nebraska Press. Copyright © 2019 by Aria Aber.

CAConrad, "[We Mention the Cat]" from "Corona Transmutations" from *Amanda Paradise Resurrect Extinct Vibration*. Copyright © 2021 by CAConrad. Reprinted with the permission of The Permissions Company, LLC on behalf of Wave Books, wavepoetry.com.

J. Mae Barizo, "New York, November" from *Tender Machines*. Copyright © 2023 by J. Mae Barizo. Reprinted with the permission of The Permissions Company, LLC on behalf of Tupelo Press, tupelopress.org.

Ellen Bass, "Sleeping with You" from *Like a Beggar*. Copyright © 2014 by Ellen Bass. Reprinted with the permission of The Permissions Company, LLC on behalf of Copper Canyon Press, coppercanyonpress.org.

Ross Gay, "Thank You" from *Against Which*. Copyright © 2006 by Ross Gay. Reprinted with the permission of The Permissions Company, LLC on behalf of CavanKerry Press, Ltd., www.cavankerry.org.

WINTER

Charif Shanahan, "Lake Zürich," from *Into Each Room We Enter Without Knowing*. Copyright © 2017. Reprinted with the permission of Southern Illinois University Press.

Noelle Kocot, "Wake Up" from *Soul in Space*. Copyright © 2013 by Noelle Kocot. Reprinted with the permission of The Permissions Company, LLC on behalf of Wave Books, wavepoetry.com.

C. D. Wright, "Poem with Evening Coming On" from *Shall-Cross*. Copyright © 2016 by C. D. Wright. Reprinted with the permission of The Permissions Company, LLC on behalf of Copper Canyon Press, coppercanyonpress.org.

José Olivarez, "The Voice in My Head Speaks English Now" from *Citizen Illegal*. Copyright © 2018 by José Olivarez. Reprinted with the permission of Haymarket Books.

Donika Kelly, "Dear— [I take the first snowfall for ash. Mistake,]" from *The Renunciations*. Copyright © 2021 by Donika Kelly. Reprinted with the permission of The Permissions Company, LLC on behalf of Graywolf Press, graywolfpress.org.

Danez Smith, "i'm going back to Minnesota where sadness makes sense" from *Homie*. Copyright © 2020 by Danez Smith. Reprinted with the permission of The Permissions Company, LLC on behalf of Graywolf Press, graywolfpress. org. Reprinted by permission of Penguin Books Limited.

"There You Are" from *Quiet: Poems* by Victoria Adukwei Bulley, copyright © 2022 by Victoria Adukwei Bulley. Used by permission of Alfred A. Knopf, an imprint of the Knopf Doubleday Publishing Group, a division of Penguin Random House LLC. All rights reserved.

"Perfect Song" from *Paper Crown* © 2025 by Heather Christle. Published by Wesleyan University Press. Used with permission. First published in *Narrative* magazine.

"These Days." By Charles Olson. Copyright © 1997 by Charles Olson Estate. Reprinted with the permission of the University of California Press Books.

"[I Won't Be Able to Write from the Grave]" from *Fanny Howe: Selected Poems*. Copyright © 2000. Reprinted with the permission of the University of California Press Books.

"Miss You. Would Love to Take a Walk with You." Copyright © 2024 by Gabrielle Calvocoressi. All rights reserved.

"Watching My Friend Pretend Her Heart Is Not Breaking" from *All the Honey* by Rosemerry Wahtola Trommer. Copyright © 2023 by Rosemerry Wahtola Trommer. Reprinted with permission of Samara Press.

Solmaz Sharif, "Self-Care" from *Customs*. Copyright © 2022 by Solmaz Sharif. Reprinted with the permission of The Permissions Company, LLC on behalf of Graywolf Press, graywolfpress.org.

Ilya Kaminsky, "Author's Prayer" from *Dancing in Odessa*. Copyright © 2004 by Ilya Kaminsky. Reprinted with the permission of The Permissions Company, LLC on behalf of Tupelo Press, tupelopress.org.

Naomi Shihab Nye, "I still have everything you gave me" from *Fuel*. Copyright © 1998 by Naomi Shihab Nye. Reprinted with the permission of The Permissions Company, LLC on behalf of BOA Editions, Ltd., boaeditions.org.

"Elegy VIII (Missing you)" by Jason Schneiderman. From *Striking Surface*, Ashland Poetry Press, 2010. Used by permission of Ashland Poetry Press. All rights reserved.

Alex Dimitrov, "The Years." Originally appeared in *The New Yorker*.

Anna Swir (Świrszczyńska), "I Am Filled with Love," translated by Czeslaw Milosz and Leonard Nathan, from *Talking to My Body*. Translation copyright © 1996 by Czeslaw Milosz and Leonard Nathan. Reprinted with the permission of The Permissions Company, LLC on behalf of Copper Canyon Press, coppercanyonpress.org.

"What is now will soon be past" from *bone* by Yrsa Daley-Ward, copyright © 2014, 2017 by Yrsa Daley-Ward. Used by permission of Penguin Books, an imprint of Penguin Publishing Group, a division of Penguin Random House LLC. All rights reserved.

Joe Wenderoth, "January 7, 1997" from *Letters to Wendy's*. Copyright © 2000 by Joe Wenderoth. Reprinted with the permission of The Permissions Company, LLC on behalf of Wave Books, wavepoetry.com.

"Winter Honey" from *Directed by Desire: The Complete Poems of June Jordan*, Copper Canyon Press © Christopher D. Meyer, 2007. Reprinted by permission of the Frances Goldin Literary Agency.

"To the Winter Apricot Blossom" from *A Cruelty Special to Our Species* by Emily Jungmin Yoon. Copyright © 2018 by Emily Jungmin Yoon. Used by permission of Harper-Collins Publishers.

"On a Train." Copyright © 2001. Used by permission of United Agents Ltd. From the book *If I Don't Know* by Wendy Cope, Faber and Faber, 2001.

"Maybe in Another Life." From *Scorched Earth* by Tiana Clark. Copyright © 2025 by Tiana Clark. Reprinted with the permission of Washington Square Press/Atria Books, an imprint of Simon & Schuster LLC. All rights reserved.

"Endings," from *The Curious Thing: Poems* by Sandra Lim. Copyright © 2021 by Sandra Lim. Used by permission of W. W. Norton & Company, Inc.

"Morning Love Poem" by Tara Skurtu. Used by permission of Tara Skurtu.

"Advice" from *The Collected Poems of Langston Hughes* by

Langston Hughes, edited by Arnold Rampersad with David Roessel, Associate Editor, copyright © 1994 by the Estate of Langston Hughes. Used by permission of Alfred A. Knopf, an imprint of the Knopf Doubleday Publishing Group, a division of Penguin Random House LLC. All rights reserved.

Wendell Berry, "To Know the Dark" from *New Collected Poems*. Copyright © 1970 by Wendell Berry. Reprinted with the permission of The Permissions Company, LLC on behalf of Counterpoint Press, counterpointpress.com.

"Letter to a Moon Child." From *Dear John, Dear Coltrane: Poems*. Copyright © 1970 by Michael S. Harper. Used with permission of the University of Illinois Press.

SPRING

"Coping," from *The Collected Poems of Audre Lorde* by Audre Lorde. Copyright © 1997 by The Audre Lorde Estate. Used by permission of W. W. Norton & Company, Inc.

"[I want to wake up]" from *How to Wash a Heart* by Bhanu Kapil. Copyright © 2020 Liverpool University Press. Used by permission of Liverpool University Press. Reproduced with permission of the Licensor through PLSclear.

"As for What the Rain Can Do" by D. A. Powell. Copyright © 2023 by D. A. Powell, originally published in *The Paris Review*, used by permission of The Wylie Agency LLC.

"I Could Let You Go." Copyright © 2014 by Thomas Dooley. Used with permission of the author.

Sean Thomas Dougherty, "Why Bother?" from *The Second O of Sorrow*. Copyright © 2018 by Sean Thomas Dougherty. Reprinted with the permission of The Permissions Company, LLC on behalf of BOA Editions Ltd., boa editions.org.

"I Need a Poem." Copyright © 2020 Kyla Jamieson. Reproduced by arrangement with Nightwood Editions. All rights reserved.

"Myth" by Ata Moharreri. Used by permission of Ata Moharreri.

"3 O'clock in the Morning" from *Black Girl, Call Home* by Jasmine Mans, copyright © 2021 by Jasmine Mans. Used by permission of Berkley, an imprint of Penguin Publishing Group, a division of Penguin Random House LLC. All rights reserved.

"Romance" first appeared in *Don't Go Back to Sleep* by Timothy Liu (Saturnalia Books, 2014).

"[You]." Jos Charles, excerpt from "May" from *a Year & other poems*. Copyright © 2022 by Jos Charles. Reprinted with the permission of The Permissions Company, LLC on behalf of Milkweed Editions, milkweed.org.

"A Cedary Fragrance" from *Given Sugar, Given Salt* by Jane Hirshfield. Copyright © 2001 by Jane Hirshfield. Used by permission of HarperCollins Publishers.

Dorothea Lasky, "I Am the Horse" from *Thunderbird*. Copyright © 2012 by Dorothea Lasky. Reprinted with the permission of The Permissions Company, LLC on behalf of Wave Books, wavepoetry.com.

Linda Gregg, "Praising Spring" from *All of It Singing: New and Selected Poems*. Copyright © 1985 by Linda Gregg. Reprinted with the permission of The Permissions Company, LLC on behalf of Graywolf Press, graywolfpress.org.

Moyra Donaldson, "What She Might Pray" from *Snakeskin Stilettos*. Copyright © 1998 by Moyra Donaldson. Reprinted with the permission of The Permissions Company, LLC on behalf of CavanKerry Press, Ltd., cavankerry.org.

"Truth is I would like to escape myself" by Nour Al Ghraowi. Previously published in *Poetry* magazine.

"Splendor" by Cole Krawitz, was originally published in *Troubling the Line: Trans and Genderqueer Poetry and Poetics*, TC Tolbert and Trace Peterson, editors. Published by Nightboat Books, March 2013.

Brenda Shaughnessy, "Miracles" from *Our Andromeda*. Copyright © 2012 by Brenda Shaughnessy. Reprinted with the permission of The Permissions Company, LLC on behalf of Copper Canyon Press, coppercanyonpress.org.

Andrea Cohen, "Orchard" from *Everything*. Copyright © 2017 by Andrea Cohen. Reprinted with the permission of The Permissions Company, LLC on behalf of Four Way Books, fourwaybooks.com.

"The Poem" from *Walking to Martha's Vineyard* by Franz Wright, copyright © 2003 by Franz Wright. Used by permission of Alfred A. Knopf, an imprint of the Knopf Doubleday Publishing Group, a division of Penguin Random House LLC. All rights reserved.

"Travelling Together" from *The Rain in the Trees* by W. S. Merwin, copyright © 1988 by W. S. Merwin. Used by permission of Alfred A. Knopf, an imprint of the Knopf Doubleday Publishing Group, a division of Penguin Random House LLC. All rights reserved.

"How to Not Be a Perfectionist" by Molly Brodak. Originally appeared in *New York Tyrant* magazine.

Caroline Bird, "Checkout" from *The Air Year*. Copyright © by Caroline Bird. Used by permission of Carcanet Press.

"Fluent" from *Conamara Blues* by John O'Donohue. Copyright © 2001 by John O'Donohue. Used by permission of HarperCollins Publishers.

Cameron Awkward-Rich, "Meditations in an Emergency" from *Dispatch*. Copyright © 2019 by Cameron Awkward-

Rich. Used by permission of Persea Books, Inc. (New York), www.perseabooks.com. All rights reserved.

Alicia Ostriker, "Don't Be Afraid" from *A Woman Under the Surface*. Copyright © 1982.

"No Romance" by Jacqueline Suskin. Used by permission of Jacqueline Suskin. From the book *Help in the Dark Season*, A Write Bloody Book, 2019.

"Scarf," from *Playlist for the Apocalypse: Poems* by Rita Dove. Copyright © 2021 by Rita Dove. Used by permission of W. W. Norton & Company, Inc.

Mosab Abu Toha, "We Love What We Have" from *Things You May Find Hidden in My Ear: Poems from Gaza*. Copyright © 2022 by Mosab Abu Toha. Reprinted with the permission of The Permissions Company, LLC on behalf of City Lights Books, citylights.com.

"For M" from *Let the World Have You* copyright © 2022 by Mikko Harvey. Reproduced with permission from House of Anansi Press, Toronto.

Gregory Orr, "[To be alive]" from *Concerning the Book That Is the Body of the Beloved*. Copyright © 2005 by Gregory Orr. Reprinted with the permission of The Permissions Company, LLC on behalf of Copper Canyon Press, coppercanyonpress.org.

INDEX OF TITLES

ABOUT THE EDITOR

The editor is a lifelong lover of words and the anonymous curator of the viral Instagram account @Poetryisnotaluxury, which has been mentioned in *The New York Times*, serves as a resource in classrooms around the world, and dedicates itself to bringing poetry to as many readers as possible.